AND OTHER
BODILESS POWERS

AND OTHER BODILESS POWERS

POEMS BY

SARAH ARONSON

newamericanpress

Milwaukee, Wis.

n e w a m e r i c a n p r e s s

www.NewAmericanPress.com

© 2019 by Sarah Aronson

Printed in the United States of America

ISBN 9781941561195

Book design by David Bowen

Cover image
"Woman Standing on Rocks in Front of the Mendenhall Glacier"
courtesy of
Alaska State Library Skinner Foundation Photo Collection
P44-11-032

For ordering information, please contact:
Ingram Book Group
One Ingram Blvd.
La Vergne, TN 37086
(800) 937-8000
orders@ingrambook.com

Many thanks to the editors who accepted the following poems for publication, sometimes with different titles or in slightly different forms:

Basalt: "Insolation (Weathering)" and "Another Poem Ending with You"

Bellingham Review: "Amalgamate"

Bennington Review: "Seam of Light through a Thicket of Nighttrees"

Big Sky Journal: "As a Consequence of Moving Forward" and "Siloed"

Boiler: "Inlet Heat"

Bright Bones: Contemporary Montana Writing: "Snowghosts, Myrrh"

Camas: "On Alces Lake"

Cirque: "Potlatch 1988"

Colorado Review: "Whiteout"

FlyFish Journal: "Open Season"

High Desert Journal: "If Not Thirst"

Inlander: "Upper Thompson River in Late Summer"

Pacifica Literary Review: "Lunar Breaks"

Portland Review: "Woman Standing in Front of the Mendenhall Glacier"

Stringtown: "Desire Line One," "Afield," and "And Other Bodiless Powers"

Yemassee: "The Auspices"

Zymbol: "Takeaways"

TABLE OF CONTENTS

*Of what advantage to me is divination
if everything is ruled by Fate?*
— Cicero

IF NOT THIRST

Then this blood-crescent welling
in a trout's small eye. The heart

so near the jaw. The water tasted
thin. I kept wrapping my hand

around my own throat. That same
spot on the river called me back.

For weeks it was meltwater
then forest fire. A patch of sun

scalping golden trees. Culling
the understory from the berries,

white spiders crawl out. A crow
from the southwest at sunset.

We exchange
in murmurations.

I take in what your good eyes
render. Press my finger to the page,

the page folds, becomes the stalk of grass
I put in my mouth to whistle you back.

DESIRE LINE ONE

I walk improvident in the direction
of a myth. A country fit for augurs

and tracklayers. Astronomers, however
imprecise. What can't be mapped: fly-thick

prairie heat. Steerless outback, pregnant
with wild sage. Again, I compare it

to the ocean. Underbelly of beetles,
alive waves. That same westering

horizon. Overhead, flyways lace.
With each scavenger wingbeat,

I make the portending good. Grid
of cottonwood. Shelterbelt.

Coming home from every direction,
plotting against what stars.

WOMAN STANDING IN FRONT OF
THE MENDHENHALL GLACIER

Warmth and recession are not to be
feared. Chattermarks in bedrock.

What if you were not my only reason
for being here? If you advance, what

might it take to surrender. Pressed
my whole torso into the wind shear,

everything felt elemental. Inside,
I could barely stand the weight

of accumulation. Downwasting
to relieve some of the pressure.

In the barren zone I could tell you wanted
to be touched, but coiled back. A cold stream

in your withdrawal. My heels
rocking in the wet footprint.

PRINCIPLES OF EQUIDISTANCE

I.

the fowl were
landlocked

                a lagoon
                backdrop

slow knotting
inner skeins

                across the strait
                seine nets heave

in pulmonary
expansion

                boundary
                waters

between where we ate
the pleiad of scallops

                my aria
                ascending

yours half-
sent back

        spit of a man
        caught

in a swell
then swallowed

        I drew the valances
        twice-over at dawn

an empty
creel

        made a balm
        for bitterness

loam and
sea spray

        pricks of brambles
        blackberry berms

II.

left to fetch
a tiger's eyelash

        for the queen
        call me

startle brow
sugar pea

        I walked
        the savage coast

retrograde
past lithic statues

        mollusks in their
        hyacinth shells

III.

I return
to the island

        opposing
        our residuum

the afternoon
a violet husk

        sagging trees
        for tincture

raked down
and under

        by an
        anchor

invoking
a bridegroom

        robed in
        fishing twine

AMALGAMATE

I surface aspirate-blue, the mother-of-pearl edging on a button blanket, cedar strips steamed then bound—a bentwood box cupping tidal foods: limpets & mussels, red ribbon seaweed & sea cucumber. Swaddled in the duff & mold of a *life-sized eagle nesting tree* before the museum is razed for asbestos & breaking fire code, where the pallor of my waist is first mentioned by the gearshift hand of a boy. I come mesomorphic, from the inherited hands of milkers, fruit pickers, the spawn of *cheechakos* who steadied a single-wide against the *williwaw*, under the loom of Thunder Mountain's chalked ridgeline— termination dust arriving each September, sometimes earlier. The season schoolchildren make fish camp, mouth *GunalchÈesh* & unflinching elocution of *strange things done in the midnight sun* under whiteout gymnasium lights to offset eighteen hours of permanent dark. The PE teacher slumps over Seagram's at the Eagle's Nest Bar, watching trawlers in Auke Bay Harbor while algae proofs the anchor chains. Tomorrow, he will set up the two-legged high kick with a whiffle ball hung from baling twine to the

backdrop of slicked-up seabirds in Valdez &
someone's father explaining how crude oil
unsettles over saline.

POTLATCH 1988

Say the fish didn't run
and the berries grew in hard.

Your traps wouldn't set
and the dye refused to take.

The blubber soured,
your woman miscarried.

Even then, you'd be spared—
called into the dim womb of cedar.

We were there too, holding
red-checked fry baskets
from the bar next door.

INLET HEAT

Meanwhile, the man in the red driver cap who fries pork spring rolls from a closet in Nugget Mall to be served at my father's fish hatchery second wedding reception, is also my soccer coach & will one day be the man playing ping pong in the driveway on my step-father's table during the only other dry day in April. All this, one hundred years after Soapy Smith put a man down at the wharf—gunshot to the groin—we laugh, my brother & I mishear Johnny Horton croon *Russia's own.* Eighty years after the Treadwell Mine caved in shoreward from where the Glory Hole's wet pit of a mouth spat up gold into the wheeling pans of *sourdoughs. Little San Francisco* ghost artists hammer driftwood into dinosaur skeletons on the single sea level drive ending out the road making in effect an island of a town with one escalator but half a dozen poured concrete corrugated-roof echo chambers for outdoor play because it is always raining & since our suits are already wet I beg Jeannie to go inlet swimming because it is static daylight at 9pm & clouds, cartridges of rain, unload only making the ocean seem warmer.

EXPIRATION BLUES

Overtones of the first and eighth elements
bound in ice—the way cold lights itself
from within. I step with my full weight
into a world. Press boots into sediment, watch
impressions swell from the ground up. Crouch
to tally the silver hairs of lupine banners,
but cannot number the soft granules in clay.
Some species flourish, come back fervid
after fire. This is certain. I say I like how suncups
dimple old snow. But this year came tundra-
sprung. Permafrost huffing, a bluff charge.

TAKEAWAYS

what begins with a wend
ends by careening

the dirt-crazed hound ignoring
high hollers to get on home

in this room we were pitiful owners
in this room are chairs for higher purpose

take everything you own
and divide it by insemination

slow down anything
and it will begin to look like seduction

stars were transiting in full view
except it was day

his finger wide enough to keep
Venus and Jupiter from marrying

hiding can only take place in pairs
there are things only two can do

STILL LIFE WITHOUT

If mother and baby feel at one,
they pulse in the red-brown glen.
Carbon copy and anima spit.

The constant setting of cries
into words. Seeking my own body
without certainty: bruise of unknown

origin. This upward-lit face. Days pass,
anhedonic as moonblindedness. Hollow
as a Chinese lantern. Tonight, art galleries

fill with mothers drinking wine. Their
babies slumped and ashen as tailings.
I etch the dandelion waiting for spring,

consider the winnowing of my old
friends. A postcard I keep forgetting
to send. The mail slot beak-tight.

IN THE VERSION I SAW

Artemisia Gentileschi paints herself in,
as I would've done. Now you say you would
be my handmaiden and do away with the head
in a basket like it was a pile of hot washings. Yes,
there were stains. A man enters and leaves
by way of the physical. I am boiling bones
down to steam. It took 87 jars of dried herbs
and a bottle of arnica to burn back the spur
that got lodged in my system. When I say sundowner,
I mean something clinical, but you think I'm talking
about a cocktail or tramp who needed a place to sleep
between trains. In the kicking daytime, I fought
my way back. Sent you down in the birdcage elevator
for strawberry tea. One can overwhelm what one loves.

SOLITUDE OF ETHER

All day women come and go from my office. *Build*
her nesting place in safety. The gloom burns off

from the waist down. Warblers hook their tiniest
songs to fog. This time of year I nurse wet hair.

New crusts of mud form around the legs
of dead grass. *The nights come to us singly. The cold*

has told me to give up. If only I could hear your voice.
Before runoff, a river otter begins wringing out dirt.

I was aloft and marching across the town's only bridge
when someone called to ask what kept my attention.

SEAM OF LIGHT THROUGH A THICKET OF NIGHTTREES

Granite dolled up
in hydrogen,

I name a planet
already named

by a man. Distend
my soft core

trying to call
your homelessness

home. Benign nevus
of my eye, how long

can I stand
on one leg?

When even my brother
is ions, blood cells,

every form of suffering.
When will I know

you won't need
a body that is mine?

Letting blood
be sap and rain

in my mouth. Take
my right hand, left

hand, turn my palms
up. Draw a card.

AFTER SCORPIO

December's first ice came stillborn. A thaw kept
calling like a relative afraid to be left out of the plans.

What's the use in mating like wolverines?
A single set of tracks leading off a cornice.

Sometimes phosphorescence, the pink orbs
of jellyfish, negate the whole plutonian seabed.

Sunday, the snow fell without consultation,
repentant as rain in the lower elevations.

Clouds untethered over the dry roads
where rooftops split the brown hills.

I HAVE A BROKEN LATCH
AND THREE LOCKS

Without which my front door wouldn't stay closed.
You step through and kiss me before looking down
to tap fresh snow from your boots. I touch the dried
white paint on your fingers and one raw knuckle,
become new ice slabbing off in the sun break.
You're the glister on the car hood.

Crossing the same bridge, I stop to watch the river
swallow ducks then spit them back up, one by one,
as if in pardon.

When the inversion returns, I'll be left with the
sparring bricks of the courthouse I pass each
morning. The line between grace and disgrace is
chalked and it is raining.

WHITEOUT

Here is the place the children
I will not have won't miss. Islands
hydrographers only suspect and so name
with doubt. The search for the neighbors
has been suspended. A year's worth
of mineral tears and debris no one
could find. How many times I also undress
to freeze on that mountainside. In dreams

I pull fistfuls of seaweed at high tide.
There are days I lumber into pine shade
so I can gaze back on the world
without squinting. On this day,
though, I would like to be delivered
to the thicket's wet center, then left.

IN KEEPING

Not a rabbit would scare itself
up. The hounds return slack-jawed,
tonguing the flat light of winter. Sweeping
the cuffs of our boots, gold vine threads
new snow. Downtrail, the village quiet
as a tinderbox. A single fox pelt wilts.
In this effortless hang of lean times,
I consider blackening my teeth with spring
bulbs. You turn your face half-away. Branches
split and hiss in the stove. For you, I translate
beingness and its opposite: berries frozen
in their store. The language of downed
trees. Still, the lake ice holds. But in keeping
ourselves upright, the mountains we imagine
are never the ones of our home.

THE 45TH PARALLEL

for Glen in Gaziantep

Raw ends of linen, we stood at the true midline
near a great seam of earth. Ripped apart, tracks

in parched dirt. A trilling canopy. We stirred
creamed honey into yogurt. I asked you to name

the body of water. Too many lakes in the brain,
you said. Now, you're talking orchids

and apricots. Makeshift counterbalances
to the assignment you were given. The border war

continues. Our father wrote sometimes work
is just that. Like taxidermy, life bears a hollow

resemblance. Animal bodies clutter every droning
highway leading out of this valley. I drive south

with the promise of new latitudes. Think of you
sketching your other hand blind. How is it

I've just found the atlas of your handwriting?

AFIELD

Compassed by lodestone,
I keep returning without
a guide. Matte of weedbed,
magpie-studded fence line.
From the bed you press me
to name all the trees. I mistake
needles on a tin roof for rain.
Your reserve of words
for vows. It is only wind
casting through the pines.

DESIRE LINES

It is February again;
light gains.

How long it took
to bury these bulbs.

Mute potential—
the hedge crusted with snow.

A bottle of liniment oil, bedside.

...

Sifting up from sleep,
something had its teeth in my hair.

The scene came tree-cut, hesitant
as a wild peacock.

A clean skiff of snow
over Moon Pass.

This dream involved fire.
Something wet caught.

I press an open hand to drywall—
permanent cold.

This isn't about you,
though you were there:

a plaid oxford,
the divot of your temple.

Why, always, this spartan climb
back into ourselves?

...

There was a time I bent down
for nothing. Had said I wanted the world

to decide. Rosemary styptic—
I talk to no one.

Ravened, and not wanting to be caught
looking like it.

A phone call from Seagoville, TX.
Vaughan Williams on the radio.

When they found her mouth
packed with earth,

I imagined sweeping
my finger through.

...

A pronghorn antler
in the Crazy Mountains,

my jacket snags swinging one leg
through barbed wire.

Strands of hair whip like tent walls.

Boot tread, the brown earth
fighting back through snow.

...

A future came to us
and we turned against it.

Plucking arrows
from the meat of our backs.

SOURCEWORK

single pip
in a cluster
of field mint
minor fissures
in ice
four parts scored
in a dark quintet
of elevations

consider these
distal beginnings
intent
on riverbed limits
scrimshaw lobes
not everything survives
as ivory

together we melt tin
pour it
into our reservoir
of snow

not everything
blooms

PLANTING IN APRIL

In asking for flushed stalks   a low swath   of rhubarb

under which   white strawberries   could seed

you shake your head   push your thumb

into a soft corner   of thyme

agree   forget-me-nots   might match the trim

say cedar   weathers to gray   I paw into loam

bees   are overtaking   the willows

the sun   blotted out   by a blurred gown   of rain

at dusk   detached bands   of ice crystals   light up

long before   other clouds   move into view

tessellations   which appear only   in the company of others

two girls   ride bikes   around the same   square block

this spring   my timing   is off

LACUNA

what arrival
moonless distention
calving generations
of shy mammals
you put ice in my mouth
to heighten the taste

CONTOUR LINE

A cairn is hunger
engineered. You take
the goat track. Visible roots
clench the lakebed. I swim out
to milk the sky. Bed down near a man
I do not know. He pleads to let his dog
sniff me, so he won't be kept awake
all night from the begging. I consider
which part of myself to offer—the ant
a single flick away. Understand,
you have been gifted this solitude
once. Does it matter I wished for loons?
The resolve of your tongue like snow.

ON ALCES LAKE

A bundle of lupine,
A morning without that insistent rooster,
A clean look at a woodpecker.

Of all the things to gift you, none
more so than that silvery trout. Half-hooked
it slipped your hand off the stern
of the canoe. We watched it sink, meter
by meter, helpless and belly-up. Glint
of scales on your palm, you paddled us back.

AS A CONSEQUENCE OF
MOVING FORWARD

The river bottom circles
your ankles downstream.

My fingers wrap around
either side of hawthorn

to steady against
runoff. Stoneflies

break into
shaky flight.

I lay orange peels
beside their split

gray husks. Lose sight of you
mending into a wide hold,

casting with the favor
of wind. I have married

a dozen fish already.
Hefted my share

of canoe. Battened on a creek,
I was only trying

to read the sky
on the water.

No, the water behind
the shadowed boulder

where an ancient steelhead
is swaying.

Swaying,
but holding.

FIR ISLAND

A guardianship of mountain passes. Three, to be exact. I came to the ocean only to have a crow steal my sock. Missed the turn-off to Fir Island and from the window imagined the side I could not see around to. In late spring we rolled our pants, let the dog loose at low tide. Her merle, rivulets of sand-wet fur, pink underbelly. The blaze of cloud. These years later what I did not expect to have misplaced was the range of another country. Orange refinery lights. In case you're feeling forgotten, tonight the tide roils at sunset where a lone kayaker bobs. I praise the mothering of bull kelp. Lift my finger to the splintering hairs of cedar bark, so ultra-soft I cannot feel them. My leg falling asleep.

INSOLATION (WEATHERING)

Nothing that happens to you in this life
is unnatural. The creek maims the road.

Border dog lamentations. A mother-cloud
and her offspring. The hands braiding my hair

are my own. Drift of javelina. Ocotillo
wags. I bend into the night half-dressed,

argue with you, fuck you rudely on the trail
in my mind. Weaken two rock slides.

What a river knows,
it channels at its deepest.

A fox gunning from the road. The price
of this aloneness is not alone. My brother

reads books on birds. Pinned against
the Flatirons, a wild donkey

screams up dawn. As if the land might stay
a language between us. Bandolier of stars.

It's sometimes difficult but I try
not to expect anything of the sky.

OPALS & ROAD SALT

Followed a desire path
in the woods—

it did not lead to water. Grip
of dewberry vine. Click and pawl.

Who do you spring for. Dawn
stung. Your quiet back

Mine is the sleep that wants to curl
toward. Nettle and blue spruce

pink the canvas of my thigh.
Snarl of map, reminds me

someone else has been here
before. The river doglegs.

I smooth barbs
as if to safety each hook.

A fist waiting
to break through.

FLIGHT PATTERNS

A warbler neck   breaks

    the band of my fingers

flits off   to yellow the sky

that spring   love

    was a washed out   road

fade lines   on the wing

jackknifing

    I couldn't   back my way

into anything

    ribbon   lightning

    trace   precipitation

a life   so minor

    that an ant   surprised me

a snake   flattened on the road

Raven's   throat

knocks   open

not just   death

     but   the   way   light

 papers   the   skin

gold   veins   the   rock

where   I   dowsed   for   you

waterline   pressing   my   thighs

     into   memory

quiet   hours   skate

above   the   creek's   din

and   me   always   calling

     from   another   epoch

Rapture   of signal fire

      earth   limits

not even her highest powers

that type   of helplessness

      that exact   hype

abstract birth defects

      promised from my phone

a week   without

      debt scare

there is not a fruit

      I care to name

side channeled

by the great animator of wind

wild rose   spook

    of moose calf

we trot   in opposite directions

 against the same thorns

SILOED

As if not everything had rusted, dry wheat
bent from seed. A split rail fence, its three crows

panting. Each mountain division was lit up
or about to be. Summer staggered,

antlers locked. Lamb's ear and mullein root
suckled. I stood beneath a lodgepole ribcage

smoke-blind. If you come back
as the sky dressed as sky,

I'll be the hacksaw,
a cricket grafting its wings.

FLATLAND

At night, cottonwoods collect vultures, bats
keening off their own nightsongs. The earth

inherited my sleep and made itself hard from it.
20 yards south of this trailer hitch bruise,

the Rio Grande bends. On a mass
of unclaimed brush, the painted turtle

suns. I, too, live in this world
unclaimed. The hair above my lip

lightens. Ocotillo flames brown.
Any water the clouds let loose

did not reach the ground. Wind
pushing my hair over the border

of that other country. Hurtle
into the current's charge. See

what washes clear. My body
will not canyon for a child.

This, and not every fish need be
caught. I never knew, Texas.

UPPER THOMPSON RIVER
IN LATE SUMMER

I.

There is a gash in the sky.
Westward, a weather system
moving in. The wind has picked up:
rain or a dry thunderstorm. The sunset lilac
from fires in Idaho. A chopper cuts
the silence, a lazy sprinkler too.

On the highway, a cow moose patrols
her just-slain calf. Blur in the rearview,
I can see the babe is all legs. The mother
false-skitters at my passing, but stays.

II.

I have moved into the pioneer cabin by the river. Banging
screen door, stale smoke upholstery. Cattle inspect then
lean against my car. A gray tabby shoots from under the
porch. On the steps, the sun-bleached skull of some
animal. Last night, the coyotes got to yipping across the
valley in stereo. There was a time we lived that kind of
ecstasy.

III.

My bones have memorized the rattle
of gate-crossing. Saddled and resigned

to the border swath. Held my breath
the night a mountain lion took down

a doe in my bootprint. Amplified sounds
of ripping, no wailing. Silhouettes

of ponderosa pines skirting the pasture.
Vanilla coming off the bark, still warm.

OPEN SEASON

On the island in the river, grasses flattened from animal sleep. Baskets emptied. Even so, I step around. Part willow switches, tilt at that same angle, then rejoin the current upstream. A killdeer wades. Persimmon leaves flash broadside in the pocket where I knew trout had been. Somewhere, a man's body reckons to limestone. A boy sights his first rifle. We draw symbols for cumulus and nimbus, build instruments for measuring wind. I lie down on the logjam knowing today the warmth of this year will end. My chest vaulted as the whitetail's ear. She will cross the river back, but only in my leaving. Only at dusk.

SNOWGHOSTS, MYRRH

The night let up downrigging. Stirred
by stinging nettles, butterscotch, the oven

heating. Standing in a carmine robe,
a gilded book covered your face. Lure

of incense, emblematic glint. Not
even icons, the pout of their lips.

When I ask you to complicate me,
I mean fasten pine boughs for pinions,

slide my hands into skinned seals.
This, a small prayer: rime seizure,

subalpine firs. That the elliptical sun
inscribe the joint where this year ends.

LUNAR BREAKS

AstrologyZone: *August is likely to be one of your very favorite months this year.*

Push the clutch in, cry.

Catch a ride to the orthopedic urgent care in a cab
in a white dress.

The woman who had the woman who had me
could have married a dentist with a temper.

No rogue planets.

Dissolve one cup sugar.
Riding my bike with one leg.

PA-C presses thumb into what is torn
is also tender. (Concern seems genuine.)

Keep hiking boots dry in an old dogfood bag
strapped to a kayak.

Muddle basil; juice of two lemons.

The leitmotif of this opera is
    insurance nearly covers the cost of people touching me.

Marry for money. Every time I see my grandmother she tells me
I have the most remarkable eyebrows.

New MD lifts one eyelid and hums *white and quiet
deep and clear*. His assistant enters into the EMR.

Has 17 unfinished charts. (Self-consciousness seems genuine.)

Didn't just stain it. Eyeliner.
Push the clutch in, drive.

Because I can't walk, can't fish.

 Five female mergansers.
 One kingfisher.

 Deep and quiet. Deep
 and clear.

Check for: tobacco dust, manifest refraction, full
or resultant acuity.

The leitmotif of this opera is
 soft tissue damage.

Fashion three gin basils.

Bid on a dinosaur bone ring.

 White
 and quiet.

Swelling down. Flexion up to 16.

I am always a patient before I am
a woman.

Release the tiny "x" valve on the inflatable kayak
to hold air.

Report from point of contact in case I don't return:
Know in your bones I will know.

THE AUSPICES

Between Wisdom and Salmon
balsam root yellows from drought.
A bittern stops for skwala. Two cranes
take off from the roadside—the labor
of awnings in twin flight. What is space for
if not longing? All these days, herons
in the water. Only crooked snags
of downed trees stalled out
in some eddy. Belly down
in six nested pools of hot water,
I dream of bee medicine. For once,
give me what I ask for: a clutch
of eggs, jeweled citrus, no wind.

ANOTHER POEM ENDING WITH YOU

Let me know when your good news
arrives, she said. First snow.

The land begins its healing.
Inlay tracks of sparring bucks—

the holding,
then the pushing back.

Name the process
by which nasturtiums endure frost.

A red-tailed hawk wheeling
over my green satin dress.

Trying always to disguise
what I most wish to say.

Another dog
barking at the night.

What we asked of each other,
only the season knew.

AND OTHER BODILESS POWERS

The ancients said anything you can't understand
is cause for celebration,
     as evidence of the mystery—
and why rain broke solid against the windshield
shutting down the interstate or why I thinned beets
in your same manner of pulling up shallow roots.

Each berry that didn't come off with a stem
stained. Hands threading and blued. What was it you called in,
transient and overtaken? A blooming vine. Fragile
as quail on the road. For a while nothing sparked.
I sat down to beads of last night's rain on stalks
of field grass. What began as a mountain range in winter

became a steelhead out of water. I had to tuck myself
into the low sway of a talus slope and by morning
gave myself to white pelicans buoying
on a warm river. Whatever crosses my path next,
let it be proof. If I am to be misled, let it be
by the first winking star, her wristlet of dust.

NOTES

"Woman Standing in Front of the Mendenhall Glacier" is after a similarly titled photograph from the Alaska State Library Historical Collections.

"Amalgamte" draws text from the Alaska State Museum website and Robert Service's *Cremation of Sam McGee*. *GunalchÈesh* is the Tlingit word for "thank you."

"In the Version I Saw" belongs to Katie Zentner and is loosely tied to the painting *Judith Slaying Holofernes*.

"Solitude of Ether" carries its title and italicized lines from the Finnish epic *Kalevala*.

"In Keeping" is after Bruegel's *The Hunters in the Snow*.

"Insolation (Weathering)" begins with an adaptation of Marcus Aurelius.

"Lunar Breaks" draws text from Susan Miller's *AstrologyZone*.

ACKNOWLEDGEMENTS

Gratitude to the steady counsel of Sherwin Bitsui and Chris Dombrowski—the rock and river respectively. This book is indebted to Joanna Klink, Sandra Lim, Greg Pape, Melissa Kwasny, Judy Blunt, Robert Stubblefield, and the rest of the University of Montana Creative Writing Program. To my closest readers: Grace Arenas, Nate Duke, Zack Rybak, Anna Zumbahlen, and Jason Santa, thank you. Thanks to The Academy of American Poets, Beargrass Writing Retreat, Fishtrap, and the Wrolstad family for their generous support.

These poems would not exist without the creative instigation of Cary Saunders, Glen Aronson, and Brock Mickelsen. To my primal and chosen landscapes, as well as my dear friends and family, you cannot know what this means. Thank you.

Born in Alaska, **SARAH ARONSON** received her MFA from the University of Montana. Her poems have appeared in *Bennington Review*, *Colorado Review*, *Yemassee*, and elsewhere. She is the host and producer of the Montana Public Radio program and podcast *The Write Question*.

CPSIA information can be obtained
at www.ICGtesting.com
Printed in the USA
BVHW062339020322
630526BV00002B/154

9 781941 561195